Delicious and He Vegan Wraps

Tasty Plant-Based Wrap Lunch Recipes

BY: TRISTAN SANDLER

Copyright © 2022 by Tristan Sandler. All Rights Reserved.

License Notes

Let's get right into it because I wouldn't say I like fluff (you will see this in my recipes):

You aren't allowed to make any print or electronic reproductions, sell, re-publish, or distribute this book in parts or as a whole unless you have express written consent from me or my team.

Why? I worked really hard to put this book together and, if you share it with others through those means, I will not get any recognition or compensation for my effort. Not only that, but it's impossible to know how my work will be used or for what purposes. Thus, please refrain from sharing my work with others. Oh, and be careful when you're in the kitchen! My team and I aren't liable for any damages or accidents that occur from the interpretations of our recipes. Just take it easy and stay safe in the kitchen!

Table of Contents

Introduction 5

1. Buffalo cauliflower wrap 7

2. Crispy tofu wrap 9

3. Caesar wrap 12

4. Hummus wrap 15

5. Spicy tofu wrap 17

6. Bean spicy wrap 20

7. Broccoli hummus wrap 22

8. Vegan sausage wrap 24

9. Mexican wrap 26

10. Lentil garlic wrap 28

11. Chickpea peanut wrap 30

12. Kale avocado wrap 32

13. Mediterranean wrap 34

14. Spicy lentil wrap 37

15. Roasted pepper wrap 40

16. Greek salad wrap 42

17. Curry chickpea wrap 44

18. Chickpea salad wrap 46

19. Mushroom wrap 48

20. Southwestern wrap 50

21. Moroccan wrap 52

22. Tahini falafel wrap 54

23. Cream cheese wrap 57

24. Greek lentil wrap 59

25. Tempeh broccoli wrap 61

26. Simple veggie wrap 63

27. Tofu wrap 65

28. Spicy chickpea salad wrap 67

29. Chipotle tofu wrap 69

30. Greek gyro wrap 71

Conclusion 74

Author's Afterthoughts 75

About the Author 76

Introduction

Becoming a vegan can be challenging for many. One of the toughest challenges is to find tasty foods that exclude unhealthy ingredients. You can quickly run out of ideas and eat the same lunch. However, being a vegan doesn't mean eating the same food. With thirty vegan wrap recipes, you will enjoy various flavors daily.

Wraps are one of the favorites of many. They are portable, so you can easily take them to work or for a picnic. On the other hand, experimenting with flavor is easy. If you are busy and don't have enough time to dedicate to cooking, this recipe book will significantly help. The best thing is that you can use convenience foods such as canned or frozen foods. With this, preparing a decent meal is straightforward. The secret is the flavor combinations, which make the vegan wrap taste excellent.

Are you ready to explore the vegan options? Let's hop on this culinary journey together!

1. Buffalo cauliflower wrap

The vegan recipe gathers a carefully chosen mix of flavors to create the best wrap. The combination of buffalo sauce and cauliflower creates a satisfying pleasure. Serve with french fries for complete enjoyment.

Time: 30 minutes

Servings: 3

Ingredients

- 3 tortillas
- 7 ounces cauliflower florets
- 3 tablespoons non-dairy milk
- ½ cup cooked brown rice divided
- 2 ½ tablespoons breadcrumbs
- ½ cup spinach
- ⅓ cup vegan cheese shredded
- 3 tablespoons Buffalo sauce divided

Instructions

Set your oven to 425 before you begin cooking.

Toss the cauliflower florets in the milk. Sprinkle with breadcrumbs on top.

Bake them for about 18 minutes.

When the cauliflower is ready, toss it with two tablespoons of buffalo sauce.

Divide the buffalo color, cheese, rice, and spinach between the tortillas. Fold both sides of the tortilla in and roll it carefully.

Add the tortilla to a heated pan and crisp it on both sides. Cut in half and serve.

2. Crispy tofu wrap

If you are tired of eating tofu the same way, this recipe will show you how to prepare this ingredient differently. The tofu dressed in a crunchy layer will become your personal favorite. It is a tasty wrap you will love, enhanced with smoked paprika.

Time: 30 minutes

Servings: 3

Ingredients

- 4 oz firm tofu
- Salt and pepper
- 2 tablespoons chickpea flour
- 1/4 teaspoon smoked paprika
- 1 tomato, sliced
- 1 avocado, mashed
- 1 red bell pepper, sliced
- 1/2 red onion, sliced
- 2 cups lettuce, sliced
- 1 tablespoon lemon juice
- 3 tortillas
- 1 tablespoon vegetable oil

Instructions

Drain the tofu and let it sit on a kitchen towel. Slice it and season with salt and pepper. Spine smoked paprika.

Add the chickpea flour to a plate and toss the tofu slices.

Heat cooking oil and fry the tofu until golden brown.

Add lemon juice, salt, and pepper to the mashed avocado and mix well.

Spread the avocado mash on the tortillas. Divide the fried tofu between the tortillas.

Divide the remaining vegetables between the tortillas.

Roll the tortilla carefully. Cut in half and serve.

3. Caesar wrap

The classic caesar salad recipe gets a vegan version, adjusted for your enjoyment. The crispy romaine lettuce with dairy-free dressing will create a tasty meal for every day.

Time: 30 minutes

Servings: 4

Ingredients

- 4 large wraps
- 2 heads of romaine chopped
- 2 avocados sliced
- 2 tomatoes sliced

Dressings

- ½ cup vegan mayo
- 2 tablespoons fresh parsley
- 2 tablespoons lemon juice
- 1 teaspoon capers
- 1 clove of garlic peeled
- salt and pepper to taste
- 1-2 teaspoons spicy mustard

Chickpeas

- 15 oz can chickpeas drained and rinsed
- ½ teaspoon smoked paprika
- ½ teaspoon onion powder
- 1 teaspoon dried parsley
- ½ teaspoon pepper
- ½ teaspoon garlic salt
- 1 tablespoon oil

Instructions

Combine the vegan caesar dressing ingredients in a blender. Pulse until smooth.

Combine the drained and rinsed chickpeas together with the seasonings. Heat the oil in a pan and cook until it is a bit crispy.

Toss the lettuce with the vegan dressing.

Divide the chickpeas, lettuce, tomato, and avocado between the tortillas. Roll the tortilla carefully. Cut in half and serve.

4. Hummus wrap

The tasty wrap gathers brown rice, spinach, and humus as delicious ingredients that perfectly match. You can choose spicy hummus if you prefer spicy foods.

Time: 30 minutes

Servings: 1

Ingredients

- 1 tortilla
- 1/4 cup brown rice cooked
- 1 cup spinach
- 1/4 cup canned beans, drained and rinsed
- 2 tablespoons hummus
- 1/2 medium carrot, thinly sliced
- 1/4 avocado, sliced
- 1/4 bell pepper, sliced

Instructions

Warm your tortilla in the microwave. Remove and spread the hummus.

Layer the remaining ingredients over the hummus.

You can cook it on a heated pan on both sides if you wish it to be crispier. Slice and serve.

5. Spicy tofu wrap

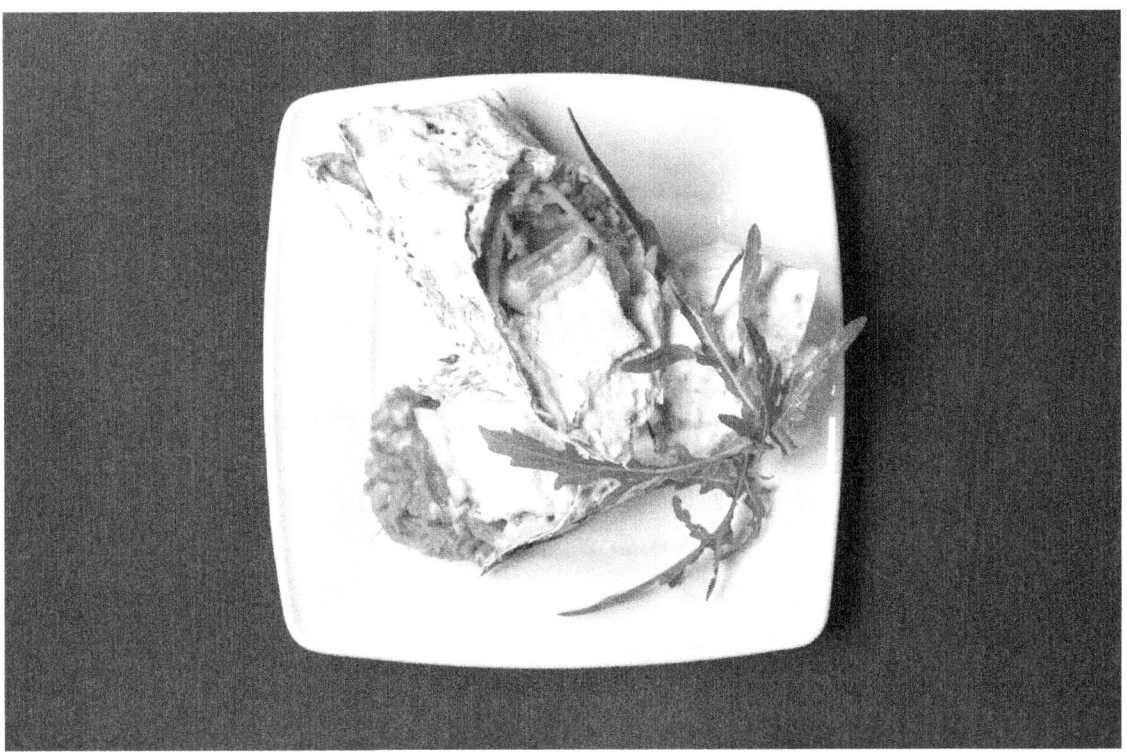

The spicy tofu wrap is an ideal pick for the ones that want to try something flavorful and exotic. Marinating the tofu is the secret trick for achieving the best flavors. This recipe reveals the perfect tofu marinade that adds tons of flavor.

Time: 30 minutes

Servings: 2

Ingredients

- 2 tortillas
- 1 cup lettuce, chopped
- 1 tomato chopped
- 1 cucumber, chopped
- 1 cup spinach
- 1 tablespoon spicy avocado sauce

For tofu

- 1 cup tofu, sliced thinly
- 1 teaspoon garlic powder
- 1 onion, chopped
- 1 teaspoon coriander, ground
- 1 teaspoon crushed red pepper
- 1 teaspoon cumin, ground
- 1 tablespoon tomato paste
- 2 tablespoons olive oil
- 1 teaspoon basil, dry

Instructions

Drain the tofu and let it sit on a kitchen towel. Heat cooking oil and fry the tofu until golden brown.

Add the remaining seasonings and stir until the tofu is covered. Remove from heat.

Divide the tofu between the tortillas. Layer the other wrap ingredients.

Roll the tortilla carefully. Cut in half and serve.

6. Bean spicy wrap

The bean salsa wrap will become your favorite when you love spicy food. However, you can always omit the hot salsa one if you wish to keep it mild.

Time: 30 minutes

Servings: 1

Ingredients

- 1 tortilla
- 2 tablespoons vegan cream cheese
- ½ cup lettuce
- 3 tablespoons canned beans, drained and rinsed
- ¼ cup sliced red pepper
- 3 tablespoons grated vegan cheddar
- 2 tablespoons hot salsa

Instructions

Spread the vegan cream cheese over the tortilla.

Layer the lettuce over the cream cheese. Top with canned beans, salsa, red paper, and cheddar.

Roll the tortilla carefully. Cut in half and serve.

7. Broccoli hummus wrap

The simple combinations taste the best. This recipe shows you how to combine simple flavors to prepare a delicious wrap ideal for a quick lunch. Broccoli ideally pairs with creamy ingredients so that a vegan yogurt would be the ideal match.

Time: 30 minutes

Servings: 1

Ingredients

- 1 tortilla
- 4 tablespoons hummus
- a few leaves of lettuce or leafy greens
- ¼ apple sliced thinly
- ½ cup broccoli slaw
- ½ teaspoon freshly squeezed lemon juice
- 2 teaspoons vegan yogurt
- salt pepper to taste

Instructions

Toss the broccoli in lemon juice, vegan yogurt, salt, and pepper.

Spread the hummus over the tortilla.

Layer the lettuce over hummus. Top with broccoli and apple.

Roll the tortilla carefully. Cut in half and serve.

8. Vegan sausage wrap

This wrap is perfect if you like vegan sausages but want to experiment with different flavor combinations. Spread with hummus and topped with cooked vegan sausage is a delicious treat after a long day.

Time: 30 minutes

Servings: 1

Ingredients

- 1 flour tortilla
- 2 tablespoons hummus
- 2 veggie sausages
- ½ onion, sliced
- 2 teaspoons oil
- ½ roasted red pepper, sliced
- Salt and pepper

Instructions

Add the vegan sausages to the heated oil and cook according to the instructions. Remove and set aside. Season with salt and pepper.

Fry the onion in the same oil.

Spread the hummus over the tortilla.

Layer the sausage and fried onion. Top with roasted pepper.

Roll the tortilla carefully. Cut in half and serve.

9. Mexican wrap

The healthy wrap recipe gathers the best Mexican flavors on your plate. The combination of beans, quinoa, and corn provides the nutrition, while the BBQ sauce adds flavor.

Time: 30 minutes

Servings: 6

Ingredients

- 6 tortillas
- 15 oz canned black beans
- 4 cups cooked quinoa
- 1 onion, chopped
- 7 oz corn
- 1 teaspoon spicy red pepper flakes
- 3 tablespoons BBQ sauce
- 1 red pepper, diced
- salt, and pepper to taste

Instructions

Cook the onion, red pepper, and pepper flakes for five minutes. Stir in the black beans and quinoa.

Add the BBQ sauce and mix well.

Divide the Mexican mixture between the tortillas. Roll the tortilla carefully. Cut in half and serve.

10. Lentil garlic wrap

Lentils are an ideal source of protein for vegans. However, you might be tired of the flavor of plain lentils. This recipe shows you how to add flavor to the lentils and enjoy them as a complete meal.

Time: 30 minutes

Servings: 4

Ingredients

- 2 cups veggie broth
- 1 cup dry brown lentils, rinsed well
- 1 teaspoon garlic chili sauce
- 3 tablespoons tahini
- 1/2 teaspoon garlic powder
- 1 teaspoon Dijon mustard
- Juice of one lemon
- 1/2 teaspoon adobo seasoning
- Salt and pepper to taste
- 1/4 cup water
- 4 tortillas

Instructions

Add the lentils to the broth in a pot and bring to a boil. Reduce to low and cook the lentils for 20 minutes or until tender. Then, drain excess liquid and set it aside to cool.

Whisk the garlic chili sauce, tahini, garlic powder, mustard, lemon juice, adobo seasoning, and water to make the sauce.

Add the prepared sauce to the cooked lentils and mix well. Divide the mixture between the tortillas.

Roll the tortilla carefully. Cut in half and serve.

11. Chickpea peanut wrap

The tasty chickpeas covered in peanut sauce will give flavor to your wrap. You can use a store-bought coleslaw mix for easy prep.

Time: 30 minutes

Servings: 3

Ingredients

- 3 tortillas
- 1 (15 oz) can chickpeas, rinsed and drained
- 2 scallions, finely diced
- 2 cups coleslaw mix

Sauce

- 2 tablespoons water
- 1 tablespoon Red Thai Curry Paste
- 1 tablespoon tamari
- 1 tablespoon peanut butter
- Juice half a lime
- 1/4 teaspoon garlic powder
- 1 tablespoon maple syrup
- 1/4 teaspoon ground ginger

Instructions

Prepare the peanut sauce by whisking the ingredients in a small bowl.

Mash the chickpeas lightly with a fork. Toss with the peanut sauce.

Layer the coleslaw mix over the tortillas. Top with the chickpea sauce mixture.

Roll the tortilla carefully. Cut in half and serve.

12. Kale avocado wrap

The kale avocado wrap creates the perfect balance between the flavors. The recipe shows you how to prepare a creamy and aromatic avocado sauce and soften the Kale for the ultimate taste.

Time: 30 minutes

Servings: 4

Ingredients

- 3 tortillas
- 1 head of kale, washed and chopped
- 1/2 cup red onion chopped
- 1 cup sun dried tomatoes
- 2 teaspoons ground cayenne pepper
- 1 garlic clove
- Salt and pepper to taste

Sauce

- 1/2 cup olive oil
- 2 tablespoons soy sauce
- 1 large avocado chopped
- 3 tablespoons nutritional yeast
- Freshly squeezed juice of 1 lemon

Instructions

Add the avocado sauce ingredients and ¾ cup of sun-dried tomatoes to a blender. Blend until smooth.

Add the kale and onion to a bowl. Toss with the cayenne pepper and the remaining ¼ cup of sun-dried tomatoes.

Add the avocado sauce to the kale and massage it to soften it.

Spread kale salad over the tortilla. Roll the tortilla carefully. Cut in half and serve.

13. Mediterranean wrap

The delicious wrap gathers the best Mediterranean flavors in the shape of a healthy lunch that is easy to make. The secret to the best flavor is to cook the chickpeas together with oil and garlic. This will release the aroma and create a flavorful meal.

Time: 30 minutes

Servings: 4

Ingredients

- 2 tomatoes, diced
- 2 cucumbers, peeled and chopped
- 1 ripe avocado, chopped
- 1 tablespoon olive oil
- Salt and pepper to taste
- 1 cup chickpeas, canned, rinsed, and drained
- 1 tablespoon olive oil
- 2 garlic cloves, minced
- 1/2 teaspoon dried mint
- 1 1/2 tablespoons tahini
- 1 teaspoon crushed red pepper
- 1 tablespoon lemon juice
- 4 tortillas
- 4 tablespoons hummus
- 1/2 cup spinach

Instructions

To make a salad, combine the olive oil, salt, pepper, tomatoes, cucumber, and avocado.

Heat one tablespoon of olive oil and fry the chickpeas over medium heat with the mint and 1 clove of garlic.

Combine the tahini, lemon juice, and one garlic clove.

Layer the spinach over the tortillas and divide the avocado salad and the tahini mixture on top.

Wrap the tortillas and cut them in half.

14. Spicy lentil wrap

If you love spicy and aromatic meals, this recipe will amaze you. However, you can also omit some of the spices if you prefer a more mild version. Either way, the aromatic lentil wraps will amaze you.

Time: 30 minutes

Servings: 4

Ingredients

- 2 cups lentils, soaked
- 4 cups water
- 1 teaspoon coriander
- 1/2 teaspoon turmeric
- 1 teaspoon red pepper flakes
- 1 teaspoon cumin
- 2 garlic cloves
- 2 tablespoons tomato paste
- 2 tablespoons hummus
- 1 tablespoon olive oil

Salad

- 1 cucumber
- 1 cup arugula
- 1 tomato
- 1 scallion
- 2 tablespoons chopped parsley
- 1 tablespoon olive oil
- 2 tablespoons chopped fresh mint leaves
- salt

Instructions

Cook the lentils in water and a little bit of salt over medium high. When done, drain them. Add coriander, red pepper flakes, cumin, turmeric, tomato paste and olive oil to the lentils and mix well. Cook until done.

Turn off the heat and add the garlic.

Toss the salad ingredients in a bowl.

Spread the humus over the tortillas. Divide the lentils and salad between the tortillas.

Roll the tortilla carefully. Cut in half and serve.

15. Roasted pepper wrap

The combination of flavors are ideal for a quick dinner. The roasted peppers fuse with the hummus and spinach, creating the ultimate pleasure after a long day.

Time: 30 minutes

Servings: 4

Ingredients

- 4 tortillas
- 1 avocado, sliced
- 2 red peppers, sliced
- 1 tablespoon olive oil
- 1/4 cup hummus
- 1/2 cup cucumbers, sliced
- 1 cup spinach
- 1/4 teaspoon garlic powder
- salt and pepper
- 1 tablespoon avocado oil

Instructions

Set the oven to 400 F and add the red peppers to the baking pan. Add olive oil over them and sprinkle garlic powder. Season with salt and pepper to taste.

Roast the peppers for 20 minutes.

Spread the hummus over the tortilla and add roasted peppers. Layer the other wrap ingredients.

Roll the tortilla carefully. Cut in half and serve.

16. Greek salad wrap

The vegan version of the Greek salad is ideal for tossing over a tortilla. Wrap it up and make a quick and easy lunch you will enjoy.

Time: 30 minutes

Servings: 2

Ingredients

- 2 tortillas
- 6 tablespoons hummus, can use flavored
- 1 cup cucumber, diced
- 3 cups baby spinach
- ¼ cup kalamata olives, roughly chopped
- ⅔ cup cherry tomatoes halved
- 2 teaspoons olive oil
- ¼ cup pepperoncini, sliced
- salt and pepper

Instructions

Spread the hummus over the tortillas.

Layer the spinach. Top with the remaining ingredients for the Greek salad wrap.

Roll the tortilla carefully. Cut in half and serve.

17. Curry chickpea wrap

The aromatic chickpea salad enhanced with curry is a tasty addition to your wrap. Enhance with crunchy veggies for complete enjoyment.

Time: 30 minutes

Servings: 5

Ingredients

- 5 tortillas
- 2½ cups spinach

Salad

- 3 cups of canned chickpeas, rinsed and drained
- ¼ cup vegan mayonnaise
- ½ teaspoon garam masala spice blend
- ¼ teaspoon turmeric
- 1 tablespoon fresh lime juice
- ¼ cup roasted cashews
- salt and pepper to taste
- ¼ cup finely diced carrot
- 1 teaspoon hot sauce optional
- 2 tablespoons freshly chopped cilantro
- 1 bell pepper chopped
- ½ cup finely diced red onion

Instructions

Lightly mash the chickpeas and add the remaining ingredients to the salad. Toss to combine the curry chickpea salad.

Lay the tortillas flat and layer the spinach. Divide the curry salad between the tortillas.

Roll the tortilla carefully. Cut in half and serve.

18. Chickpea salad wrap

The simple recipe shows you how to veganize the famous chicken salad. The mashed chickpeas add protein, while the other ingredients add flavor.

Time: 30 minutes

Servings: 4

Ingredients

- 4 tortillas

Salad

- 15 oz canned chickpeas, drained and rinsed
- 2 tablespoons vegan mayo
- 1/4 cup red onion diced
- 2 tablespoons minced dill
- 2 tablespoons minced parsley
- 1/3 cup celery sliced
- 1/8 cup chopped walnuts
- 1/4 cup purple grapes halved
- 1 tablespoon Dijon mustard
- Salt and pepper

Instructions

Add the drained chickpeas into a bowl and mash them lightly with a fork. Combine all the ingredients for the chickpea salad.

Divide the chickpea salad between the tortillas.

Roll the tortilla carefully. Cut in half and serve.

19. Mushroom wrap

When you love mushrooms, the mushroom wrap is all you need. If you prefer a lighter version, you can switch the flour tortilla with a gluten-free version or simply wrap the filling in lettuce.

Time: 30 minutes

Servings: 4

Ingredients

- 4 tortillas
- 24 oz brown button mushrooms diced
- 1/3 cup fresh cilantro leaves
- 3 scallions thinly sliced
- 1 tablespoon sesame seeds

Sauce

- 2 tablespoons rice vinegar
- 1/2 cup tamari sauce gluten-free
- 2 tablespoons maple syrup
- 2 tablespoons creamy peanut butter
- 1 teaspoon red pepper flakes
- 1 teaspoon ground ginger
- 1 teaspoon garlic powder

Instructions

Cook the mushrooms with a little bit of water over medium heat. Add salt. Cook until the liquid evaporates, and they are done.

Combine the peanut sauce ingredients in a bowl.

Toss the cooked mushrooms in the peanut sauce.

Divide the mushroom between the tortillas. Roll the tortilla carefully. Cut in half and serve.

20. Southwestern wrap

The southwestern wrap gathers authentic flavors, coming in a vegan version to suit your needs. The combination of ingredients is perfect, while you still get to feel the hint of lemon.

Time: 30 minutes

Servings: 4

Ingredients

- 4 tortillas
- 1 ½ tablespoons of vegan butter
- 1/4 cup red onion diced
- 1/4 cup red bell pepper diced
- 15 ounces corn from a can, drained and rinsed
- 3 garlic cloves minced
- 1 teaspoon of chili powder
- Juice of ½ lemon
- Salt to taste
- 1 (15 oz) black beans from a can, drained and rinsed
- 1 Avocado sliced

Instructions

Heat the butter and cook the pepper and onion for two minutes.

Add the corn and garlic and cook for five minutes.

Add lemon juice, beans, salt, cilantro, and chili.

Layer the avocado slices over the tortillas and divide the pepper mixture. Roll the tortilla carefully. Cut in half and serve.

21. Moroccan wrap

The Moroccan wrap gathers oriental flavors, creating a simple and easy meal you can prepare during weekdays. The addition of apricots and pistachios adds an exotic element to this meal.

Time: 30 minutes

Servings: 4

Ingredients

- 1/2 cup cooked whole wheat couscous
- 1/4 teaspoon smoked paprika
- 1 cup spinach shredded
- 4 large whole wheat wraps
- 1/4 cup pistachios minced
- 1/4 cup apricots sliced
- 1/4 cup green olives sliced
- salt and pepper to taste

Salad

- 3 tablespoons vegan mayonnaise
- 1 (15 oz) can chickpeas drained and rinsed
- 1/2 teaspoon turmeric
- 1 teaspoon harissa or to taste
- 1/2 teaspoon smoked paprika
- salt and pepper to taste

Instructions

Add the chickpeas to a bowl and lightly mash them with a fork. Add the remaining Moroccan salad ingredients and mix well.

Layer the other ingredients over the tortilla. Top with the Moroccan salad.

Roll the tortilla carefully. Cut in half and serve.

22. Tahini falafel wrap

A tasty falafel wrap smothered with tahini is a guilt-free meal that will satisfy your cravings. The secret to preparing the best falafel is to enhance it with lots of spices.

Time: 30 minutes

Servings: 4

Ingredients

- 4 tortillas
- 1 cup mix of chopped tomato and cucumber

Falafel

- 1 (15 oz) can of chickpeas, drain and save the aquafaba
- 1 tablespoon of chickpea liquid or aquafaba
- 2 cloves garlic, chopped
- 1 teaspoon ground coriander
- ¼ onion, diced
- 2 tablespoons chopped fresh parsley
- 1½ teaspoons ground cumin
- ⅛ teaspoon cayenne pepper
- ½ teaspoon baking soda
- 3 tablespoons chopped fresh cilantro
- 1 teaspoon salt
- 1 tablespoon of freshly squeezed lemon juice
- 1-2 teaspoons of Extra-Virgin olive oil
- Pepper

Dressing

- ¼ cup tahini
- 1 tablespoon hot water
- 3 tablespoons lemon juice
- 2 tablespoons minced shallot
- 2 tablespoons chopped fresh parsley
- 2 garlic cloves, chopped
- Salt and pepper to taste

Instructions

Set the oven to 350 F.

Add all the ingredients for the falafel to a food processor and pulse until you have a thick mixture.

Scoop 12 balls on a paper-lined baking sheet and bake them for 20 minutes.

Combine the tahini dressing ingredients and mix them well.

Layer the falafel and tahini over tortillas. Add tomato and cucumber and serve.

23. Cream cheese wrap

The vegan cream cheese wrap is the ideal pick when you don't have time for cooking. Add the creamy dairy-free cheese over the tortilla and layer the veggies. You can even customize this simple recipe to your liking and use different veggies.

Time: 10 minutes

Servings: 1

Ingredients

- 1/4 cup baby spinach
- 1 tortilla
- 2 tablespoons dairy-free cream cheese
- 1/2 ripe avocado, sliced
- 1/4 sliced cucumber cup thinly
- 2 tablespoons red onion, minced
- 1/2 tomato, thinly sliced
- Salt and pepper

Instructions

Spread the vegan cream cheese over the tortilla.

Layer the other ingredients on top.

Roll the tortilla carefully. Cut in half and serve.

24. Greek lentil wrap

The combination of Greek salad and lentils creates the perfect fusion of flavors. The sun-dried tomatoes add unique flavor, while the vegan pesto adds aroma.

Time: 10 minutes

Servings: 1

Ingredients

- 1 tortilla
- ¼ cup vegan cheese cubed
- 1/2 cup lettuce torn
- 2 tablespoons basil vegan pesto
- 3 tablespoons sun-dried tomatoes in oil
- 1/4 cup cooked lentil

Instructions

Spread the pesto over the tortilla. Arrange the ingredients over it.

Roll the tortilla carefully. Cut in half and serve.

25. Tempeh broccoli wrap

If you like tempeh, this recipe is for you. The cooked tempeh fits perfectly in combination with broccoli and vegan yogurt.

Time: 30 minutes

Servings: 6

Ingredients

- 6 tortillas
- 1 pound tempeh, sliced and cooked
- 2 cups broccoli, steamed
- 1 cup vegan cheese
- 1/2 cup vegan yogurt
- salt and pepper

Instructions

Spread the vegan yogurt over the tortilla.

Layer the broccoli and tempeh slices. Top with vegan cheese and seasoned with salt and pepper to taste.

Roll the tortilla carefully. Cut in half and serve.

26. Simple veggie wrap

The simple veggie wrap is an effortless meal that you can put up within 10 minutes. You can use homemade or store-bought hummus, depending on the time you have.

Time: 10 minutes

Servings: 4

Ingredients

- 4 tortillas
- 1 cup hummus, can use spicy if preferred
- 1 avocado thinly sliced
- ½ large cucumber sliced
- 1 bell pepper thinly sliced
- 1 large tomato sliced
- 1 small carrot julienned
- 1 cup lettuce torn to pieces

Instructions

Spread the hummus over the tortillas.

Arrange the avocado, cucumber, pepper, tomatoes, carrot, and lettuce.

Roll the tortilla carefully. Cut in half and serve.

27. Tofu wrap

The tasty tofu with a peanut sauce is ideal for vegans experimenting with flavors. You can roast the cubed tofu to achieve the perfect crispiness.

Time: 30 minutes

Servings: 4

Ingredients

- 6 tortillas
- 3 cups coleslaw mix
- 1 cup shredded carrots
- 1/3 cup roasted peanuts
- 1/4 cup chopped fresh cilantro
- 2 cups tofu cubed

Sauce

- 1/4 cup honey
- 3 tablespoons rice vinegar
- 1/4 cup peanut butter
- 1/4 cup olive oil
- 1/4 teaspoon red pepper flakes
- 1 tablespoon soy sauce
- Salt and pepper
- 1 large garlic clove, minced
- 1 tablespoon grated fresh ginger

Instructions

Combine the peanut butter sauce ingredients in a small bowl.

Add the coleslaw, cilantro, carrots, and peanuts to a salad bowl. Toss them with the sauce.

Layer the peanut butter sauce salad over the tortillas. Top with cooked tofu.

Roll the tortilla carefully. Cut in half and serve.

28. Spicy chickpea salad wrap

Chickpea is the go-to ingredient for tasty creamy salads. This version is spicy and hot but has an abundance of flavors.

Time: 20 minutes

Servings: 2

Ingredients

- 2 tortillas
- 4 oz canned chickpeas
- 2 teaspoon hot sauce of your preference
- 1 teaspoon soy sauce
- 1 1/2 tablespoons vegan mayonnaise
- 1/2 cucumber, thinly sliced
- 2/3 cup carrots shredded
- 1/2 avocado, thinly sliced

Instructions

Mash the chickpeas gently with your fork.

Add the hot sauce, soya sauce, and vegan mayonnaise. Mix well to combine the salad ingredients.

Divide the spicy chickpea salad between the tortillas. Top with avocado slices, carrots, and cucumber.

Roll the tortilla carefully. Cut in half and serve.

29. Chipotle tofu wrap

The roasted tofu enhanced with chipotle will add a special touch to this meal. You can use spicy hummus if you prefer so.

Time: 1 hour 10 minutes

Servings: 4

Ingredients

- 4 tortillas
- 1 1/4 cups hummus
- 1 1/3 cups cooked quinoa
- 1 cup diced cucumber
- 1 cup bell pepper diced
- 1 cup leafy greens

For tofu

- 12 oz extra firm tofu, drained, dried and cubed
- 3 tablespoon olive oil
- 1/2 teaspoon garlic powder
- 3/4 teaspoon chipotle powder
- 1/4 teaspoon ground cumin
- salt

Instructions

Toss the tofu in oil and spices.

Arrange the seasoned tofu on a paper-lined baking sheet and bake in a preheated oven to 415 F for 50 minutes or until crispy. Flip them halfway.

Spread the hummus over the tortilla.

Layer the other scrap ingredients. Top with cooked tofu.

Roll the tortilla carefully. Cut in half and serve.

30. Greek gyro wrap

The Greek gyro is a traditional dish typical of this Mediterranean country. This veganized version gathers the best favors but keeps them vegan.

Time: 30 minutes

Servings: 4

Ingredients

- 4 tortillas
- 1 medium tomato, sliced
- Half cucumber, sliced thinly
- 1/2 small red onion, thinly sliced
- 3 cups leafy greens
- 4 tablespoons vegan tzatziki sauce

Tofu

- 12 oz of extra firm tofu, drained, dried and cubed
- 2 tablespoons oil
- 2 tablespoons balsamic vinegar
- 3 tablespoons tamari
- 1 tablespoon tomato paste
- 2 tablespoons brown sugar
- 1 teaspoon salt
- 1/2 teaspoon granulated garlic
- Pepper
- 1/2 teaspoon ground coriander
- 1/2 teaspoon dried dill
- 1/4 teaspoon cumin
- 1/2 teaspoon dried oregano

Instructions

Toss the tofu in oil and spices.

Arrange the seasoned tofu on a paper-lined baking sheet and bake in a preheated oven to 415 F for 50 minutes or until crispy. Flip them halfway.

Arrange the tortillas with sliced vegetables and greens. Add the tofu on top.

Finish With tzatziki sauce. Roll the tortilla carefully. Cut in half and serve.

Conclusion

When you have the healthy vegan wrap recipe book in your hands, consuming delicious vegan food is very easy. You learned how to add flavor to vegan wraps. Also, these recipes teach you how to prepare a delicious meal using convenience foods. You won't need to spend your money on lunches now. You can prepare a tasty wrap and take it to work. You will feel satisfied and complete with the balanced mix of veggies and beans. The healthy ingredients will provide you with all the nutrients you need while letting you enjoy the flavors.

This wasn't just an ordinary recipe book but a significant step towards a meaningful life change. If you like this collection of recipes, don't mind checking the others. We have an extensive collection of cookbooks, so you will find the right fit for your needs!

Author's Afterthoughts

thank you

Now's the moment of truth… What did you think about my cookbook? Did you like the recipes in it? While I certainly hope so, I would also like to know what you'd like to see more of! This might come as a surprise to you, but your ideas will surely inspire my upcoming cookbooks since the only reason I write is so that you can try out my dishes! Without you, I certainly wouldn't be here–writing and all.

Perhaps you'd like a cookbook to help you with weight loss or to help you stick to the Keto diet while eating delicious meals…Or maybe you'd just like to see a whole cookbook on brunch recipes or overnight breakfasts… You're the boss!

The only reason I can write cookbooks and try new recipes for a living is because of you, so now is my time to show some gratitude by creating cookbooks that will actually help you get through your weekly meals or special occasions! Just let us know what you'd like to see more of, and you can bet we'll get your ideas to the drawing board.

Thanks,

Tristan

About the Author

Tristan grew up watching his dad and grandma spend hours in the kitchen before a family gathering. They would prepare some of granny's secret family recipes together and then serve them once everyone arrived. Tristan only chopped carrots and onions for them, occasionally stirring the pots too, but he didn't realize how important his job was until he grew up and found himself needing a hand in the kitchen.

Especially when living on your own, doing all the chopping and cooking yourself can be very tiring. While he wished his cat could lend him a paw, hairballs weren't exactly part of his weekly night menu. For some time, Tristan lived off take-out food because it was convenient. After a long day of work, who wants to spend another hour preparing dinner and then washing the dishes? It wasn't until a buddy of his, who also happened to live on his own, introduced him into the world of meal preps and easy, simple dinners that Tristan's life changed.

He started cooking for himself. Nothing fancy, just quick but healthy meals that didn't make him dread coming home to make dinner. The cleanup was easy, too, since it was mostly one-pot meals. Eventually, he started to freeze his meals for the entire month, only reheating them as needed. His colleagues started to pick up on this, and they were soon asking Tristan to make their weekly lunch and dinners too!

Though he never envisioned himself as a full-time cook, Tristan now runs his own meal prep company in California, preparing over 1,000 meals per week for busy people who want healthy homemade meals. Occasionally, his dad goes to help out in the kitchen, now only letting him chop carrots and onions, occasionally stirring the pots too, and Tristan can't believe how lucky he is to have a helping hand like his.

Printed in Great Britain
by Amazon